Illustrated
Stories *from the* Bible

Volume 3

AUTHORS
George and Marilyn Durrant
Former Professor of Ancient Scriptures

Educational Doctorate

ARTIST AND ART DIRECTOR
Vernon Murdock
Artist Illustrator

Bachelor of Fine Arts
Graduate Work, University of Madrid,
*   Spain*

CORRELATORS AND DIRECTORS
Steven R. Shallenberger, *President*
Community Press, Wisdom House, Eagle
*   Marketing Corporation*

Bachelor of Science; Accounting, Business.
SCMP, Graduate School of Business, Harvard
*   University.*

Paul R. Cheesman
Director of Scripture in Religious Study Center
Chaplain, U.S. Navy

Doctor of Religious Education

Lael J. Woodbury
Chairman, National Committee on Royalties,
*   American Theatre Association*

Doctorate of Theater, University of Illinois

ADVISORS
Dale T. Tingey
Director American Indian Services and
*   Research Center*

Doctor of Philosophy, Guidance and
*   Counseling; Washington State University*

Reverend Raymond E. Ansel
Ordained Minister

Southwestern Assemblies of God College, Texas
*   Berean Bible School, Missouri*

Millie Foster Cheesman
Writer, Poetess

M.J. Bardon
Missionary-Pastor, Grace Baptist Church

Th. M. Clarksville School of Theology
*   Clarksville, Tennessee*

Reverend William R. Schroeder
United Church of Christ

United Theological Seminary of the Twin Cities
*   New Brighton, Minnesota*

Copyright © 1980 by
EAGLE SYSTEMS INTERNATIONAL
Library of Congress Catalog Card No.: 80-80314
ISBN: 0-911712-63-1

SECOND EDITION VOLUME 3, 1981

Lithographed in U.S.A.
by
COMMUNITY PRESS, INC.
P.O. Box 1229
Antioch, California 94509

A member of
The American Bookseller's Association
New York, New York

Now therefore fear the LORD, and serve him in sincerity and in truth: and put away the gods which your fathers served on the other side of the flood, and in Egypt; and serve ye the LORD.

And if it seem evil unto you to serve the LORD, choose you this day whom ye will serve; . . . but as for me and my house, we will serve the LORD.

Joshua 24:14, 15

Smilax: a climbing plant found in the Holy Land. It has broad shiny evergreen leaves, small greenish-yellow flowers, and red berries. The young shoots are eaten like asparagus.

Dedicated to boys and girls throughout the world and to all who love the Bible.

A non-denominational work.

CONTENTS

Our story so far . . .

In the first two volumes we read of the glorious creation of the earth. We learned of Adam, Noah, and the tower of Babel. The great prophet Abraham, his son Isaac, and his grandson Jacob were discussed.

In these volumes we came to understand God's great love for his children and learned of the promise he made to Abraham, Isaac, and Jacob, that through them and their children he would bless all the people of the world.

In Volume Two Jacob wrestled all night with an angel and his name was changed to Israel. Esau forgave Jacob and allowed him to return to the Promised Land.

Our hearts were saddened to see Jacob's son Joseph sold into Egypt by his brothers. Joseph refused to give up and, after interpreting Pharaoh's dream, became a great leader in Egypt. He forgave his brothers and they and father Jacob came to live with Joseph in Egypt.

On the pages that followed a baby was born who was meant to have been destroyed by the wicked Egyptians. He was protected and saved in an exciting way by a wise mother, a loving sister and the Lord. That baby boy grew up and became the mighty prophet Moses.

Then came the battle of wills—Moses against Pharaoh. Finally, after many horrible plagues, the Israelites were free to leave Egypt, although it took still another miracle (the parting of the Red Sea) to finally rid them of the Egyptians. They then left on their hard, long journey into the desert wilderness.

As the nation of Israel journeyed, manna came from heaven, enemy armies were defeated, a tabernacle was made of canvas, and the Ten Commandments were given.

Yes, we have learned much of the Lord and of his love for his children from the first two volumes. Now we will see how Israel struggles with other problems and after forty years finally enters the Promised Land.

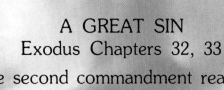

A GREAT SIN
Exodus Chapters 32, 33

The second commandment reads: "Thou shalt not make unto thee any graven image. . . ." Would a statue of a young cow made of gold and worshipped by the people be a graven image? Indeed it would. Such an image was made by the very people who only a short time before had seen God's miracles.

How could the Israelites be so quick to forget the second commandment? It happened like this. Moses went up on the mountain to pray, to learn, and to be taught by God. Because God had so many things to tell him, Moses was gone for forty days.

During the first week the people didn't miss Moses much. They worshipped God and kept his laws. Then the trouble began. Some of the leaders, remembering the golden gods the Egyptians worshipped, asked all the people to give them their golden jewelry. These precious things were melted and an artist made the gold into a large golden calf.

It was such a beautiful statue that all the people bowed down and worshipped it as the Egyptians had done. Aaron was soon doing as the others and even built an altar in front of the image. This seemed perfectly natural since this was the way the Egyptians had taught them to worship.

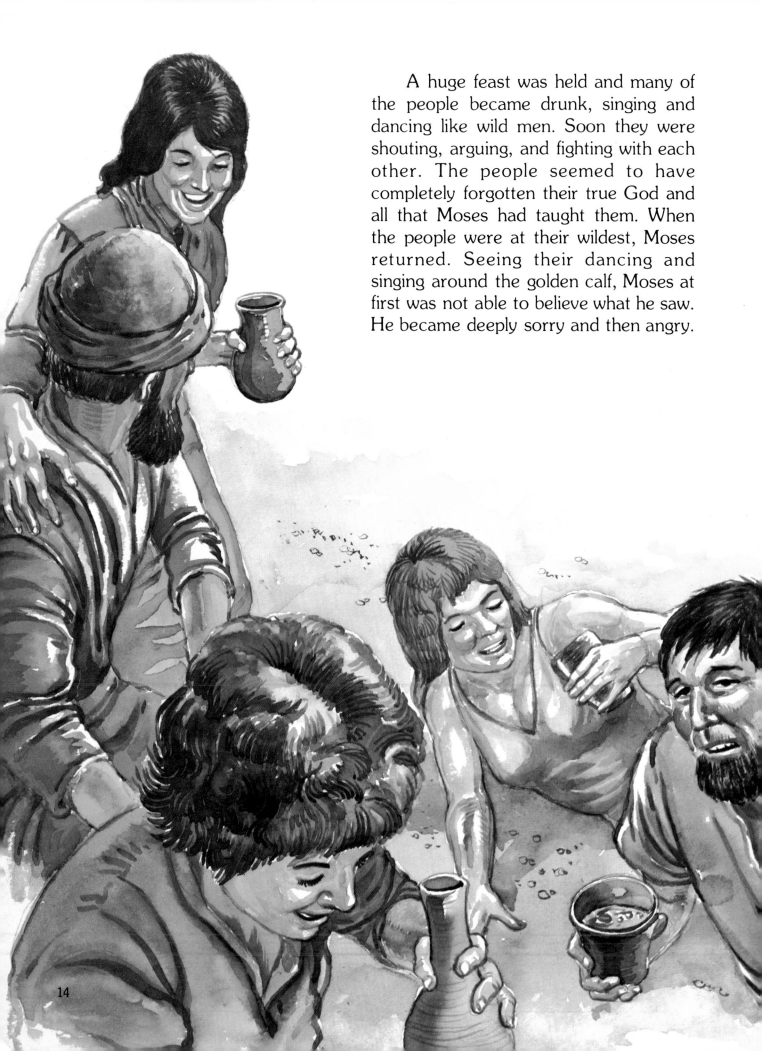

A huge feast was held and many of the people became drunk, singing and dancing like wild men. Soon they were shouting, arguing, and fighting with each other. The people seemed to have completely forgotten their true God and all that Moses had taught them. When the people were at their wildest, Moses returned. Seeing their dancing and singing around the golden calf, Moses at first was not able to believe what he saw. He became deeply sorry and then angry.

14

"And he took the calf which they had made, and burnt *it* in the fire. . . ." How was it possible for one man to make all those people back away while he destroyed their golden god? When people are doing wrong, they are weak. When Moses appeared, the people felt guilty and did not dare to fight him.

Aaron made excuses, saying, "We didn't know if you would ever return. We were discouraged. We didn't think it would matter." But it did matter and Aaron knew it. He was suddenly ashamed and so were all the other people. They begged Moses to forgive them.

Moses was angry at what his people had done, but he loved them. He went to the Lord and asked the Lord to forgive them. He then told the Lord that if the people couldn't be forgiven, he would like to be punished along with them. He felt responsible for his people, who had suffered so much in Egypt as well as in the wilderness.

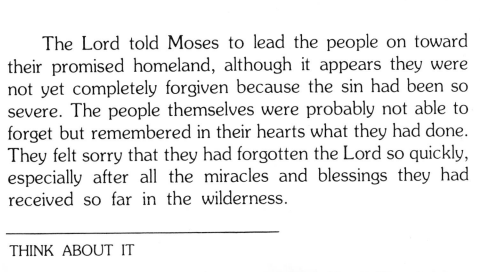

The Lord told Moses to lead the people on toward their promised homeland, although it appears they were not yet completely forgiven because the sin had been so severe. The people themselves were probably not able to forget but remembered in their hearts what they had done. They felt sorry that they had forgotten the Lord so quickly, especially after all the miracles and blessings they had received so far in the wilderness.

THINK ABOUT IT

1. What can we learn from the story of the golden calf?
2. Disobeying God brings much unhappiness. What is the best way to be happy?

THE TWELVE TRIBES OF ISRAEL

Those people who went out of Egypt with Moses are often called the "children of Israel," even though many of them were grown-ups. Since they were adults, why were they called children? Perhaps since all of them had lived as slaves, none of them had ever had a chance to make any important decisions. As slaves they had almost

always been told what to do and how to do it. Now they were no longer slaves, yet because of their past experience, they didn't know how to make wise decisions. Heavenly Father knew that these Israelites were not a strong group of people. That is why Moses didn't lead them in a straight path from Egypt to the Promised Land, or the land of Canaan as it was called. If they had gone directly to their new home, that would have taken only a few days. Instead, Moses was prompted to spend some time in the wilderness to let his people get used to being free. They needed time to get ready for the hard battles they would have to fight to win back the cities and the land that had been given by Heavenly Father to Abraham, then to Isaac, and finally to Jacob (whose name God had changed to Israel).

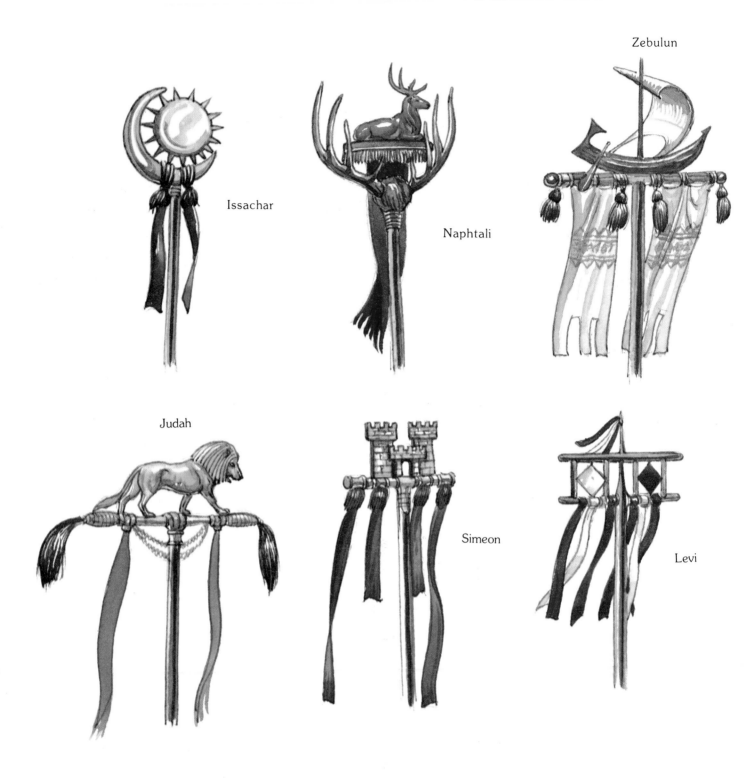

Issachar

Naphtali

Zebulun

Judah

Simeon

Levi

Because of these reasons Moses didn't lead his people straight ahead to the Promised Land. Instead he kept them in the desert, or wilderness, for more than a year. Then, feeling that the people were ready, he was prompted to lead them to a place near the southern borders of what would much later be their home.

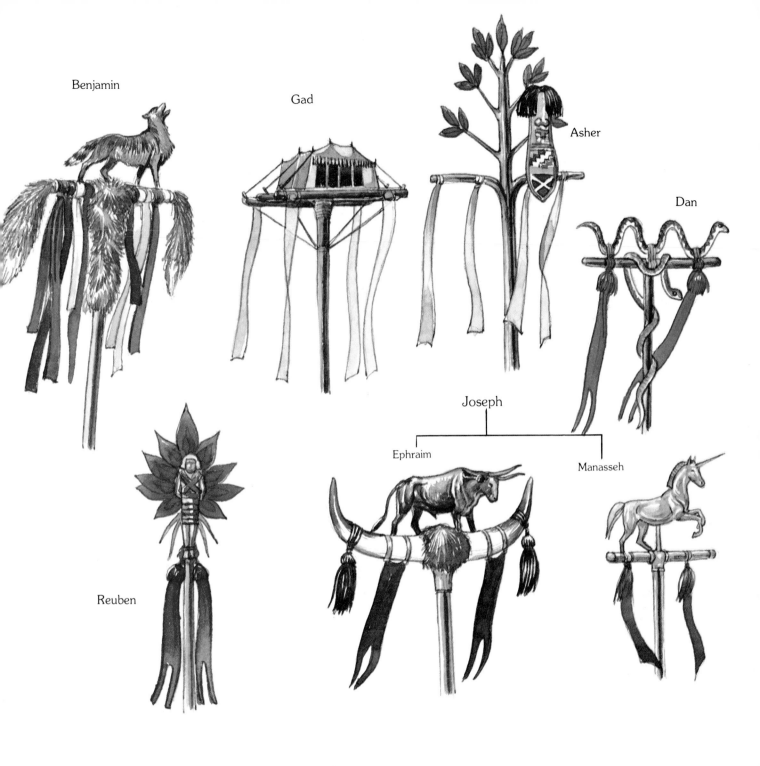

Benjamin

Gad

Asher

Dan

Joseph

Ephraim

Manasseh

Reuben

At this time there were so many children of Israel they were called a nation. The nation of Israel was divided into family groups called tribes, each tribe being made up of descendants from a son or grandson of Jacob (Israel). It was the people from all these tribes (or large families) that Moses was leading to the Promised Land.

21

GETTING ORGANIZED
Numbers Chapter 13

Moses decided that he should find out more about the Promised Land before he led his people there. He wondered, "Are the people who live there strong? Do they live in big cities? Do they have armies? Can we win a war against them?" To find the answers to these questions, he decided to send a group of men secretly into the land as spies. Because he wanted the people in each tribe to feel they were part of the future plans, he chose one man from each of the twelve tribes. These twelve men were to be the first to see their new home. They would need to be very careful though, for if they were discovered they would be killed.

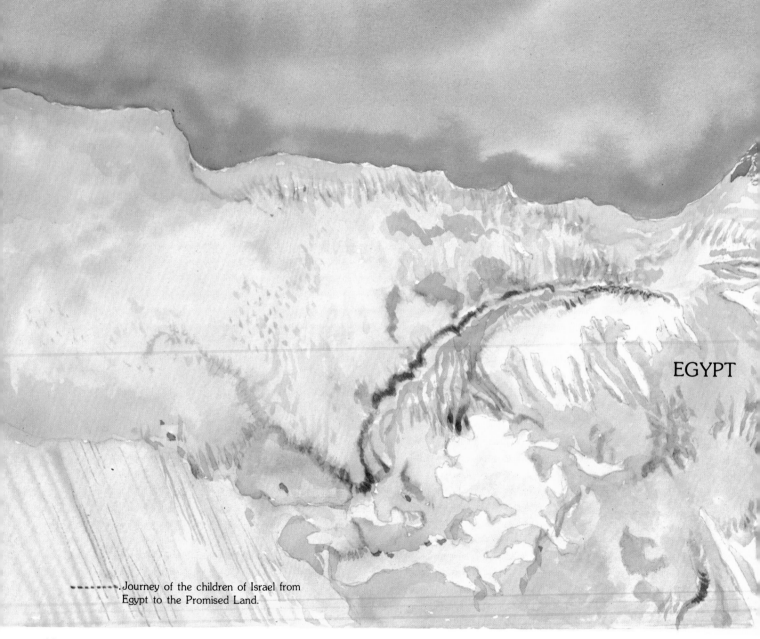

EGYPT

- - - - - - - Journey of the children of Israel from Egypt to the Promised Land.

GREAT SEA

Mt. Hermon ▲

Tyre •
Dan •   Bashan

Hazor •

Acco •

Sea of
Chinnereth

Gilead

Mt. Tabor ▲

Megiddo •

Jezreel •

Joppa •

Rabbah •

Heshbon •
Mt. Nebo ▲

Jericho •

Jerusalem •

Ammon

Salt Sea

Hebron •

Moab

Gaza •

Philistines

Arad •

Beersheba •

Wilderness
of Zin

Kadesh-
barnea •

Edom

Raamses
(Avaris) •

Zilu •

Wilderness
of Shur

Goshen

Succoth •

Pithom •

* Reed
Sea (yam Suf)

Wilderness
of Paran

Bitter
Lakes

Ezion-
geber
Elath •

Memphis •

Midian

(Ras Sudar) •

Marah •

* Elim •
(WadiFiran)

Rephidim •

* Mt. Sinai ▲
(Jebel Mussa)

(Sharm E. Sheikh)

RED SEA

MURDOCK

23

*These place names are the names used in Moses' day and
many have since been changed.

Joshua and Caleb were among the twelve who listened with excitement as Moses said, "And see the land, what it *is*; and the people that dwelleth therein, whether they *be* strong or weak, few or many." After being taught by Moses, the twelve daring spies left on their secret mission.

A REPORT OF FEAR AND OF FAITH
Numbers Chapters 13, 14

For over five weeks Moses and his people waited. During this time they probably wondered, "When will the twelve men come back? What if they don't come back? What if they are captured?" Then, after forty-five days, a loud and happy shout filled the air: "They are back! The spies are back!" The crowds of people that gathered were amazed as they looked at the large cluster of grapes being carried on a pole by two of the newly returned heroes. "Look at that," some said in hushed voices. "How was it in the land?" others asked anxiously. The quick reply by one of the tired but excited spies was, "Just look at this fruit and you will know for yourselves."

Moses quickly sent word to the leaders of each tribe that a meeting was to be held. At this gathering the spies reported on their secret mission. While the others listened almost breathlessly, one man, speaking for ten of the men, told those listening that the land "floweth with milk and honey; and this *is* the fruit of it. Nevertheless the people *be* strong that dwell in the land, and the cities *are* walled, *and* very great. . . ." He added, "And there we saw the giants . . . and we were in our sight as grasshoppers, and so we were in their sight."

After the report had ended, some of the people were filled with fear and began to cry. They shouted: "There is no hope! We have come all this way and now there is no place to go. We could never conquer giants who live in cities surrounded by high walls." In anger they shouted at Moses, "Why did you bring us here? We don't want to be here. We wish we had died in Egypt." From these statements one can understand how these people were not very mature.

Joshua and Caleb, the other two spies, tried to calm the people. They enthusiastically said, "We saw the land and it is beautiful. The people there are big, but if the Lord is with us, we can conquer them. We must have faith." But the people wouldn't listen. Reaching down, they picked up stones and threw them at the two faithful spies.

It must be remembered the Israelites had been slaves all their lives. They needed still more time to be taught and to build a strong faith. Because they were weak and unwilling to go to battle, the Lord told Moses to lead his people back into the desert. Little did Moses or the people know at this time that their fear would cause them to remain another thirty-nine years in the desert. By the time these thirty-nine years were over, all those who had been adults when they left Egypt would be dead. Of this group only Joshua and Caleb, the two faithful spies, would set foot in the Promised Land. Even Moses, their great prophet, would die before the Israelites would settle in their God-given home.

THINK ABOUT IT

1. Ten of the spies said, "We can't do it. They are giants and have walls around their cities. We can't win a war against them." Joshua and Caleb said, "We know it will be hard, but with the Lord on our side we will win." Who was right?
2. Which of the spies had faith and which had fear?
3. What is the difference between faith and fear?

THE PRIESTHOOD OF GOD

Life in the wilderness was hot, dry, and discouraging. However, the Lord helped the Israelites find water and food. The people also had a tabernacle, in which to honor God, and a great prophet to lead them. For these reasons life wasn't without its happy moments, even while living in tents amidst the blowing sands of the desert wilderness.

Aaron made mistakes in his life but felt sad about these sins. This caused him to change, or repent, and from then on he did many good things. God is pleased with those who feel sad about their mistakes and want to change and keep all his commandments. Thus he was very happy with Aaron. Moses was told by God to give him a blessing that would make him the great high priest. After that blessing Aaron's work was to take care of the tabernacle and do the work necessary to help the people worship in the tabernacle. Aaron's sons helped him in the work, which was called the work of the priesthood. Later Aaron's grandsons also helped.

Time passed and one sad day Aaron died. Because of their sorrow the people mourned for thirty days. All their memories of Aaron were good ones, and they knew in the days ahead they would miss their great high priest. Fathers and mothers told their children about the olden days when Aaron had spoken to help Moses in his struggles with the wicked Pharaoh. They told them how he had helped to hold up the arms of Moses so that the armies of Israel could win. These stories excited the children and they also grew to love Aaron. All the people were glad when the son of Aaron, whose name was Eleazar, was chosen as the new high priest. They hoped he would be a great leader, just as Aaron had been.

The name of Aaron is still a name that most people know. When people read the Bible they learn that, although Aaron had problems, he repented and was forgiven by God and was loved by his brother Moses and all of the people. It is inspiring to know that, like Aaron, anyone can change and please God as Aaron did. When this happens, God will allow that person to help him with his work on the earth.

THINK ABOUT IT

1. Aaron once made a mistake. How do we know that after he changed, or repented, God forgave him?

Cyclamen: This plant is found in rocks, walls, and edges of thickets in Palestine. It is the wild parent of our cultivated winter-flowering cyclamen.

LISTEN TO THE PROPHET'S VOICE
Numbers Chapter 21

Aaron wasn't the only one of the children of Israel who died during the forty years spent wandering in the great wilderness between Egypt and the Promised Land. In fact, at least one million people died and were buried under the desert sands.

Some died horrible deaths—like those bitten by snakes that slithered into the big tent city of Moses and his people. Screams were heard all through the day and night, as men, women, and children were bitten by the poisonous serpents.

To try to protect themselves, the people took sticks and stones to beat on the crawling, poisonous enemies. But soon they cried, "It is no use. We kill one and ten more seem to appear right out of the ground. We are doomed!"

In desperation those Israelites who had been unkind to Moses went to him and begged, "We have sinned, for we have spoken against the LORD, and against thee; pray unto the LORD, that he take away the serpents from us. And Moses prayed for the people. And the LORD said unto Moses, Make thee a fiery serpent, and set it upon a pole: and it shall come to pass, that every one that is bitten, when he looketh upon it, shall live."

At first the people probably said, "Moses is foolish. How can looking at a metal snake wrapped around a pole help us recover from the bite of a deadly snake?" Then someone actually did as Moses had said and was healed. Thus all those with faith in Moses' words looked at the serpent of brass and, by obeying, they lived.

Moses may have told the people that someday the Son of God would be lifted up on a pole or cross. All that looked upon him with faith would be freed from the poison of their sins. Some 1500 years later Jesus said, "And as Moses lifted up the serpent in the wilderness, even so must the Son of man be lifted up: That whosoever believeth in him should not perish, but have eternal life."

The story about the serpents is
a good example of how problems
can creep and crawl into anyone's
life. But if people will do as the Lord
tells them to do, they will be protected and live a happy life on the earth;
and because of Jesus, all people
may have eternal life in heaven.

THINK ABOUT IT

1. Today we are not usually bothered by snakes, but Satan sends other things to try to destroy
   us. What are some of those things?
2. Jesus and the prophets tell us what to do to avoid the bad things Satan tries to send into our
   lives. If we are to be protected from these sins, what must we do?

BLESSES INSTEAD OF CURSES
Numbers Chapters 22-28, Deuteronomy Chapters 31-34

Time passed—ten years, then twenty, then thirty. The long years in the wilderness were about to end. The children of Israel had been given a chance to grow up through their experiences, learning to be dependable and making their own decisions. They were more obedient than they had ever been before. Now they were ready to enter the Promised Land of milk and honey, giants, walls, and enemy armies. However, this time they went forward with faith instead of fear.

They had many miles to travel and needed to go through that part of the wilderness where other people lived. One king, who saw the Israelites coming, sent them a message, saying, "I will not allow you to cross my land!" To back up his message he sent an army to punish the Israelites. To his surprise his army was soon crushed by the army of Moses. The Israelites were indeed no longer as children.

Another king, a giant named Baskan, became angry when he learned of Israel's victory. He was certain his army could destroy the wanderers from the desert. But the Israelites received strength from God and soon destroyed both the giant king and his army.

Word has a way of traveling fast. Soon all the small kingdoms in the area had heard of Israel's victories. Panic came into their hearts as they thought, "God is with these people. They will come into our land and destroy us." One king named Balak felt that his only hope was to get God to be on his side instead of on Israel's. He decided to hire a prophet of his own who could call down God's power to curse Israel.

Such a prophet was known to be living in a land some miles away. Balak sent some of his men to go to the prophet and offer him money to come and say a prayer that would cause God to curse Moses and his people. When Balaam, the man of God, heard the offer, he refused. He did not want any part of cursing those whom he knew were God's chosen people.

The messengers returned to Balak and said, "Balaam won't come." Balak became very angry. He gave his servants orders to return to Balaam, this time to offer more money and to promise him that he would gain great honor if he would come and curse Israel. This temptation was too much for Balaam. He decided to at least go and see what would happen. Little did he know as he left his home that he was headed right into a strange adventure.

As the small donkey carrying Balaam made its way over the desert sand, it suddenly turned aside, left the path, and pushed against a wall. Balaam's leg was almost crushed and he shouted angrily as he gave the poor animal a hard blow. Twice more the little beast stopped. Balaam grew even more angry and hit the donkey each time his usually obedient friend stopped.

Suddenly something happened that had never happened before. The donkey turned its head toward its master and spoke. Its words were, "What have I done unto thee [Balaam], that thou has smitten me these three times?" The donkey added, with some sorrow, that it had always been a good and faithful donkey. It must have felt it was being treated very unfairly, for speaking was a most unusual thing for an animal to do. Truly the Lord had put words into the donkey's mouth.

Balaam felt both amazed at what he had heard and sorry for his good little friend. Then the prophet looked up and saw what the donkey had seen that had made it stop. There, standing in the path, was an angel of the Lord with a sword in his hand. The angel told Balaam that the Lord was not pleased to see Balaam on his way to curse God's people. The old prophet felt bad and quickly said, ". . . I will get me back again." But the angel told Balaam to continue on and, instead of cursing Israel, to bless them. So that is what he did. You can imagine how angry this must have made Balak the king; yet there was nothing he could do about it. As Balaam departed for home, he probably smiled, feeling happier that he could bless God's people instead of curse them.

THINK ABOUT IT

1. Do you feel that Balaam was a good man? Why?
2. Why did he finally agree to go with Balak's servants?
3. What does this story teach us about the temptations of glory, honor, and money?

A SAD BUT HAPPY DAY
Numbers Chapter 27, Deuteronomy Chapters 31-34

Much has been said about Moses, but now he was nearly 120 years old and about to die. Knowing that he must soon leave his beloved people, Moses worried about their future. He wondered, "Who will lead them through the hard battles that must soon be fought? Who will help them to defeat the giants who live in the walled cities of the Promised Land?" Moses spent much time in prayer.

As Moses prayed, the Lord spoke and told him, "Take thee Joshua the son of Nun, a man in whom *is* the spirit, and lay thine hand upon him." Moses did as the Lord told him. He placed his hands on Joshua and, with the power of God, gave Joshua the power and authority to be the next prophet and leader of the Israelites. Thus Joshua, who thirty-nine years earlier (along with the faithful spy Caleb) had wanted to enter the holy land, was now to do just that. Because he had been faithful for so many years, he became the leader who would see millions of Israelites finally enter their promised land.

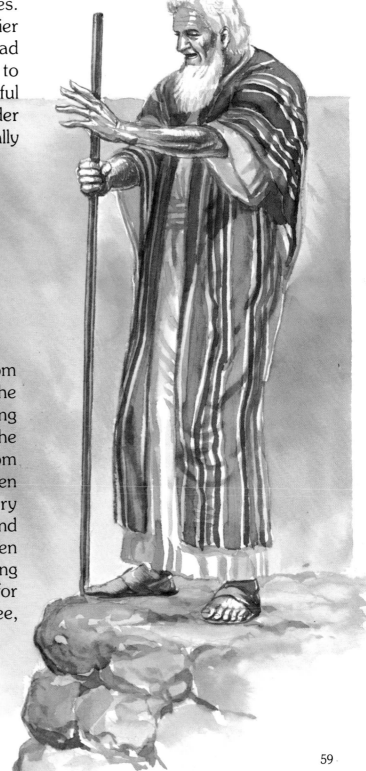

In a final speech to the people whom he loved, Moses reminded them of the many things that had happened during the past forty years. He mentioned the opening of the Red Sea, the manna from heaven, the Ten Commandments written by the finger of God, and the fiery serpents. He told them to be faithful and to choose to live good lives. He then blessed Joshua by saying, "Be strong and of a good courage, fear not . . . for the LORD thy God . . . will not fail thee, nor forsake thee."

The work God had given Moses to do was now finished. Moses knew that the time had come to leave his people for the last time. Alone, he walked away from the thousands of tent homes, from the beautiful canvas tabernacle where so much had happened, and from the beloved children of Israel. As he did so, he may have paused and looked back one final time, hoping and praying that God would continue to be with his people.

A short time later, from the top of Mount Pisgah, Moses was able to look at a distance. There he saw the Promised Land—the land given to Abraham, to Isaac, to Jacob, and now to Joshua. After the Lord had told him that all would be well with his people, this great prophet, who had lived to free his people and to teach them God's laws, died. There he was taken by the Lord, who said of him, "And there arose not a prophet since in Israel like unto Moses, whom the Lord knew face to face."

"And the children of Israel wept for Moses . . . thirty days." Moses had indeed been a great leader and a mighty prophet.

THINK ABOUT IT

1. What do you feel made Moses the great man that he was?
2. Joshua had wanted to enter the Promised Land but couldn't because the people were not prepared. Did he give up because he had to wait? What can we learn from Joshua about patience?

61

IT CAN BE DONE
Joshua Chapters 1-3

Joshua must have missed Moses, but there was no time to look back when they could look forward to so much. The tents that made up the nation of Israel were now on the east bank of the beautiful Jordan River. The walled city of Jericho was on the other side. How were the Israelites going to cross the river and conquer such a strong fortress as Jericho? This was the question in Joshua's mind and he had to find an answer. He knew that there was great

honor and glory in being a leader, but there was also the heavy burden of responsibility. However, Joshua knew that whenever God gives responsibility, he also gives the power to do all that is asked. God spoke to Joshua and said, ". . . go over this Jordan, thou, and all this people, unto the land which I do give to them, *even* to the children of Israel. . . . There shall not any man be able to stand before thee all the days of thy life: as I was with Moses, *so* I will be with thee: I will not fail thee, nor forsake thee. Be strong and of good courage . . . for the LORD thy God *is* with thee whithersoever thou goest."

With such promises how could Joshua fail? He now felt he could cross
any river and win any battle, his faith was so fixed and strong. Although
Joshua knew that God would help, he also knew that he must first figure it out
and plan to do all that he could himself. As he planned, he decided to send two
spies into Jericho. That night the two spies swam across the cool waters of the
Jordan and crept quietly across the flat ground that led to the city gate. They
entered the city and silently made their way to a small inn.

A woman named Rahab, who worked at the inn, knew who the spies were and told them she wanted to help them. Then someone knocked on the door. It was soldiers who had heard that two strangers were in the city. They asked where the two men were. Rahab, hearing the voices of the soldiers,

quickly led the spies up the stairs to the roof. There she had them lie down while she covered them with stalks of flax. Then she hurried back and told the soldiers that the two men had been there but they had departed. She pointed down the street. The soldiers hurried away in the direction Rahab sent them.

Returning to the two spies, she said, "I know that the LORD hath given you the land, and that your terror is fallen upon us. . . ." She told them that she had heard about the Red Sea and all the other miracles that had helped the Israelites. She then asked them to promise her that, because of her kindness to them, they would not harm her or her family when they destroyed Jericho. The men were most grateful for her help and promised that they would indeed deal kindly with her and her family in the future.

Walls of Jericho

"Then she let them down by a cord through the window: for her house *was* upon the town wall, and she dwelt upon the wall." Before going, they told her to leave the red cord dangling from her window so that the Israelite army would know the house where Rahab's people lived and would spare them.

Hand over hand, the spies made their way to the ground. They then ran into the hills and hid. After three days they felt it was safe, so they crossed the river and went straight to Joshua.

With great excitement they told him the story, saying, "Truly the LORD hath delivered into our hands all the land; for even all the inhabitants of the country do faint because of us." Joshua must have felt happy to know that the people of Jericho and all of the land were afraid. It is much easier to defeat people who are afraid than those who have faith.

The time for the invasion was drawing near. Joshua spoke to his people and said, "Sanctify [purify] yourselves: for tomorrow the LORD will do wonders among you." That night each family probably knelt in prayer. Children might have asked, "What did Joshua mean?" Parents perhaps answered, "We are not sure, but we think tomorrow we will enter the Promised Land." There was most likely little sleep that night on either side of the mighty Jordan River.

THINK ABOUT IT

1. Would you like to have been Joshua during these exciting times? Why?
2. What did the spies accomplish in Jericho? What did this have to do with faith and fear?

THERE IS A WAY
Joshua Chapters 3, 4

Early in the cool morning air there was much excitement in the Israelite camp as tents were taken down and packed for the move. The descendants of Aaron, who were from the tribe of Levi, hurriedly took down the sacred canvas tabernacle. Quiet conversations took place among each family, and each group was asking such questions as: "How will we cross the river?" "Will there be a boat?" "Will there be a bridge?"

Honored men carried the sacred box, which was called the ark of the covenant. It contained the most holy things the Israelites owned. Joshua told these priests to walk toward the Jordan River, which was wider than normal, being at the flood stage.

75

We are not sure what was in the minds of the people as they watched the priests approach first the mud line and finally the water's edge. Perhaps the priests themselves wondered about their own fate; but they believed Joshua was like unto Moses, and if he said "go forward," they would go forward in faith.

Just as the feet of the two priests in the lead were about to touch water, something happened that left the priests, the people, and even Joshua breathless. The river stopped, as if blocked off by an invisible dam. As a large wall of water formed the priests continued forward, walking on ground where the river had been.

As the Israelites' hearts pounded anxiously, over one million of them crossed the path that led across the bottom of the Jordan River. Stories that had been told to these Israelites by their parents about the crossing of the Red Sea now flashed back into their minds. The God of Israel was indeed an all-powerful and almighty God.

When all were across and safe on the western shore, twelve large stones were brought from the riverbed and made into a memorial. This monument would help them remember for a long time that when God gives a commandment, he will always provide a way for it to be accomplished.

THINK ABOUT IT

1. Why should we never forget this story about the Israelites crossing the Jordan River?
2. If we are faithful and obedient to God and do everything in our power to solve the problems we face, what will happen?

THE LORD IS OUR CAPTAIN
Joshua Chapter 5

Joshua knew that God had helped them cross the river, but that was in the past. As Joshua walked into the hills, he looked at the walls of Jericho, and wondered about the future. How could this walled city best be taken? Perhaps he was thinking of ordinary ways—like climbing up the walls or breaking down the gates.

While he thought of what he should do, a most wonderful thing happened. ". . . he lifted up his eyes and looked, and, behold, there stood a man . . . with his sword drawn in his hand. . . ."

Pomegranate: The pulp from this fruit has been used in drinks and sherbets since the days of Solomon. The rind and flowers were used as dye.

Joshua, who thought he had been alone, must have been startled at seeing this stranger. He walked over to him and asked, "*Art* thou for us, or for our adversaries [enemies]?" The man replied, "Nay; but *as* captain of the host of the LORD am I now come."

83

Joshua suddenly knew he was standing in the presence of a heavenly being who had been sent to assure him that the Lord would go before the armies of Israel. He would help them win the battles that would secure for them their Promised Land.

Joshua fell to his knees, worshipped God, and asked, "What saith my lord unto his servant?" The captain of the Lord's host then told Joshua what had been told Moses some forty years earlier at the burning bush: "Loose thy shoe from off thy foot; for the place whereon thou standest is holy. And Joshua did so."

God really does live and he will help anyone who is doing the right thing. If a person is strong and refuses to give up, is willing to struggle again and again with his problems, and will ask the Lord, he will be with him. The Lord will be the captain who will help that person win any battle he faces.

DO IT THE LORD'S WAY
Joshua Chapter 6

Once the Israelites had crossed the river, no one came out from Jericho and no one went in. The people inside the walls were in a state of fear. Joshua and his army were ready to attack but still needed the Lord's plan.

The Lord revealed to Joshua his strange plan of attack. Once each day for six days a very special march was to be carried out. First would come the army of Israel, followed by seven priests blowing their trumpets or rams' horns. Behind the trumpeters would come the ark of the covenant, carried on the shoulders of several priests. Last of all would come a special guard.

The Israelites walked silently around the entire city. Those inside were completely confused by this strange and mysterious march. All that could be heard was the muffled sound of feet marching and the mournful sound of the rams' horn trumpets. After circling the city one time, the priests and the army returned to their camp.

Thus they continued marching around the walled city once a day for six days. The seventh day dawned. This was to be the day! Those inside watched as the unusual march circled the city once. But what was happening? Instead of going back to their camp the army was circling the city again and again, marching seven times around the city. Then through the long silence came the deafening sound of the priests blowing on their ram's horns. On that signal every Israelite shouted as loudly as his or her lungs would allow. The earth seemed to shake. Suddenly cracks appeared in the walls and stones began to tumble. Everywhere the walls of Jericho were collapsing.

After a few crushing, crashing, screaming moments, the mighty city of Jericho lay in a mass of rubble and ruin. The battle, if it can be called such, was over. Israel had taken the first city in their new homeland, although it wasn't much of a city anymore. Only the kind woman Rahab and her family were still alive. The two spies had gone back and brought them and their possessions out of Jericho. Then Joshua warned his people, "Cursed *be* the man before the LORD, that riseth up and buildeth this city Jericho. . . ."

THINK ABOUT IT

1. It has been said that God's ways are not man's ways. How does the story of the battle of Jericho prove this statement?
2. What do you think caused the walls of Jericho to fall?

NO POWER IF YOU DISOBEY
Joshua Chapter 7

God wanted his people, the Israelites, to have the land, but he didn't want them to have the cities, the gold, the silver, or the animals. They could build their own cities and produce their own riches. They had their own animals. That is why God told Joshua his people should not take any of the treasures or riches of Jericho.

One soldier named Achan, however, entered a crumpled house and saw some beautiful clothes and gold and silver. He knew he shouldn't take them, but he really wanted them. He quickly picked them up and hid them in his bag. After looking around, he felt safe because no one had seen what he had done—no one, that is, but God.

The next battle to be fought was against the little city of Ai. It appeared that it would be an easy battle because it was not a strong city. Yet something went wrong and the Israelites were defeated. Joshua was saddened and amazed as he thought, "Has the captain of the Lord's hosts forgotten us?"

Joshua was so discouraged that he laid down on the ground and cried as he prayed. God spoke, saying, "Get thee up . . . Israel hath sinned . . . they have even taken of the accursed thing . . . and they have put *it* even among their own stuff."

Joshua then knew why his army had lost the battle of Ai. God went on to tell his great prophet about what Achan had done. Achan then confessed his sin to Joshua. Because this was such a serious crime, Achan was stoned to death.

Joshua had told his people that God wanted them to have only the land. They must not take any of the possessions. Joshua was also told by the Lord that the Israelites must destroy all the people in order for them to be able to worship God in peace in this land forever. But Satan, who had been the one who told Achan to disobey God, had other ideas. He would do all he could to keep the Israelites from having the Promised Land to themselves.

PRAY TO KNOW THE TRUTH
Joshua Chapter 9

Then a trick was pulled on Joshua. Some men from a city called Gibeon got some dry, moldy bread, put it in their packs, and came wandering down the road into the Israelite camp. They were taken to Joshua and, when asked who they were, they said, "We have come from a far distant city. See this old bread. It was just out of the oven when we left home and now it is moldy."

Joshua and his men probably thought, "They have really come a long way. Their city wouldn't even be in the Promised Land." The strangers asked Joshua to promise never to harm them or their city. Joshua agreed, not realizing they had actually come only a few miles from their city. Satan had helped these people make up their lies. He is clever and plays tricks on anyone who will believe him.

Joshua was sad when he heard the truth about who the strangers were. Now these people would have to be allowed to stay in the Promised Land. God's plan for his people to be the only ones in this holy land was not turning out that way. Satan was working hard to keep the land from being a place where God's people could live and become a blessing to all the world, as God had promised.

Why did Joshua make such a mistake? The Bible mentions that when Joshua had heard the story of these strangers, he believed them because he ". . . asked not counsel at the mouth of the Lord." In other words, Joshua had gone on his own judgment and had forgotten to pray about it. None of us are wise enough to always find the truth without God's help. People should rely on their own judgment, but only after they have prayed. They must do their part and then the Lord will help them with the answer.

THE SUN OBEYS
Joshua Chapter 10

Remember that God created all things, including the sun and the moon, thus even these mighty heavenly bodies obey him. One day a great battle was being fought between the Israelites and an enemy army. The Israelites were winning and had a chance to destroy the entire army, but to do this they needed more daylight. It was then late afternoon and darkness would soon come. If the enemy could hold out a little longer, the sun would go down and they could escape into the blackness of night.

As the enemy army retreated, Joshua watched the sun gradually sink lower in the western sky. After speaking with the Lord, he shouted out, "Sun, stand thou still. . . . And the sun stood still. . . ." In the light of this miraculously long day Joshua and his army completely destroyed the enemy. God, desiring his people to have this choice land to themselves, had caused the sun to stand still. God truly is all-powerful.

Most of the battles were now over, although there were still groups of Philistines and other tribes of defeated people scattered about. Joshua and his army thought that these few people couldn't possibly cause any problems and so they were left alone. However, they would indeed cause problems in the future, as will be seen.

The Lord had promised to give this holy land with its beautiful Jordan River, its salty Dead Sea, its fertile valleys, and its lofty mountains to his people. Now, as he had promised Abraham, Isaac, Israel (Jacob), Joseph, Moses, and Joshua, the land of Canaan was once again the homeland of God's chosen people

At this time Joshua sent word to his people that a great meeting was to be held. Leaders from each tribe were invited. At this meeting the land of Canaan (the Holy Land or the Promised Land) was divided into twelve parts.

The Israelites were divided into twelve small state-like territories that together formed one great nation. These territories were created when the land was divided and assigned to twelve family groups, called tribes, all but two of the tribes being named after the sons of Jacob (Israel). There was the tribe of Reuben, Simeon, Judah, Issachar, Zebulun, Dan, Naphtali, Gad, Asher, Benjamin, Ephraim and Manasseh (the latter two, Ephraim and Manasseh, were sons of Joseph, who was the son of Jacob).

Another tribe, descended and named after Levi, the third son of Jacob, had been chosen by the Lord to be his special priesthood holders. Thus the tribe of Levi had been divided up and lived among the other twelve tribes and therefore did not have a separate portion of land.

When people speak about the twelve tribes they are usually referring to the twelve land tribes rather that the tribes of the actual sons of Jacob (Israel).

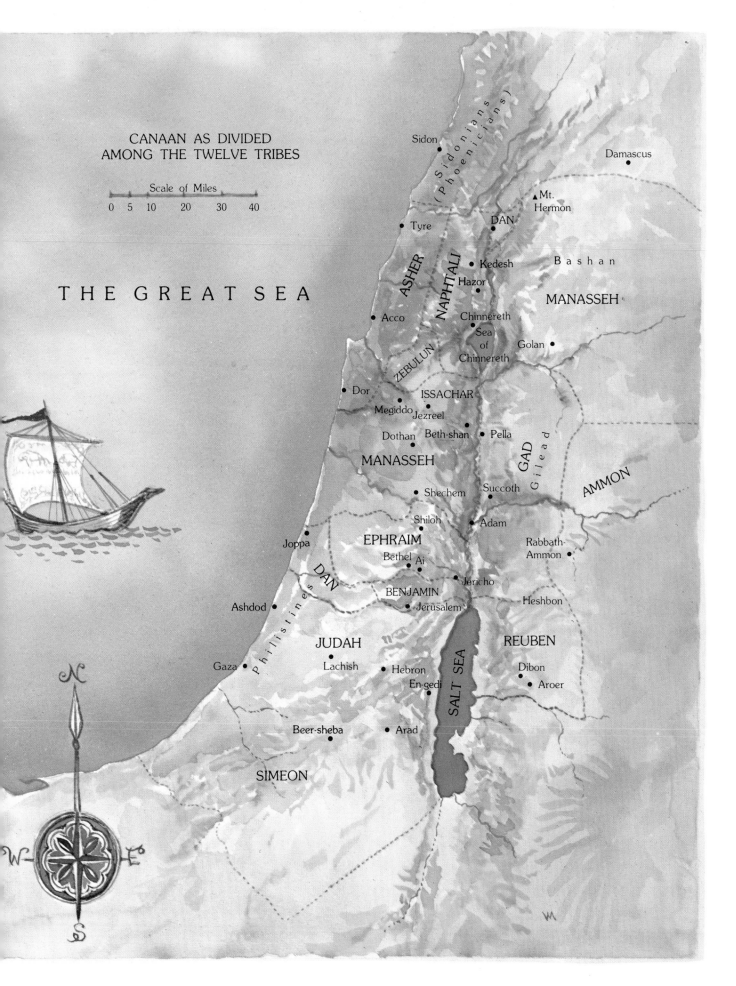

CANAAN AS DIVIDED
AMONG THE TWELVE TRIBES

Scale of Miles

0   5   10   20   30   40

THE GREAT SEA

Sidon

Damascus

(Sidonians Phoenicians)

Mt. Hermon

Tyre

DAN

Bashan

Kedesh

ASHER

NAPHTALI

Hazor

MANASSEH

Acco

Chinnereth

ZEBULUN

Sea of Chinnereth

Golan

Dor

ISSACHAR

Megiddo

Jezreel

Dothan

Beth-shan

Pella

GAD

Gilead

MANASSEH

AMMON

Shechem

Succoth

Shiloh

Adam

EPHRAIM

Rabbath-Ammon

Joppa

Bethel   Ai

DAN

Jericho

BENJAMIN

Heshbon

Ashdod

Jerusalem

Philistines

JUDAH

REUBEN

Gaza

Lachish

Hebron

Dibon

En-gedi

SALT SEA

Aroer

Beer-sheba

Arad

SIMEON

N

W   E

S

109

Joshua's work was now done and he had seen his dream come true. He gathered his people together to give them his last great message, which was ". . . serve him [the Lord] in sincerity and in truth: and put away the gods which your fathers served . . . in Egypt; and serve ye the LORD. And if it seem evil unto you to serve the LORD, choose you this day whom ye will serve; . . . but as for me and my house, we will serve the LORD."

Joshua had been asked by God to perform a large task. This he did, thus serving the Lord. If only everyone would say, as Joshua did, "As for me and my family, we will serve the Lord."

THINK ABOUT IT

1. The Lord is always willing to help us, but we must do our part. What is our part?
2. Why could the Lord stop the sun?

SATAN CAUSES BAD SEEDS TO GROW

The people were deeply saddened when their great prophet and general, Joshua, died at the age of one hundred and ten. They remembered his words and served the Lord for many years. Then trouble began to creep in, as Satan continued to try to destroy all the good Joshua had done.

The Israelites built many cities and many of them were no longer herdsmen as they had been in the wilderness. There were still battles to be fought because there were still many Canaanites to be driven out of the land, but the Israelites were tired of war. Besides, they could see no reason to fight against these people who were not causing them any problems.

Little did they know that these people who worshipped golden statues were the very seeds that Satan would use to cause God's people so much sadness. As time went by, many Israelites disobeyed God, married the Canaanites, and began to serve the strange gods of these people. The Israelites, who had been so strong under Joshua and with God at their side, began to grow weaker. The Canaanites began to gain power over them. Now that it was too late, the Israelites could see why God had commanded them to destroy all of these people.

THINK ABOUT IT

1. Why didn't the Lord want the Israelites to take any of the treasures or riches of Jericho?
2. Why didn't he want them to mix with the people who already lived in the Promised Land?
3. What did all this have to do with the promise God had given his people that they would be a blessing to all nations?

114

A WOMAN INSPIRES ISRAEL
Judges Chapter 4

Things had changed for the worst. They always do when God is disobeyed. The Canaanites who lived in the Promised Land had once been afraid of the Israelites. Now it was just the opposite—the Israelites had become weak and now they feared the Canaanites.

For twenty terrible years a war raged in the Promised Land. The Canaanite army fought against Israel and, after many battles, almost totally defeated God's people. The Israelites, though not willing to change and become obedient to God, hoped and prayed for help. In their prayers they asked God for help, saying, "Please send us a great leader such as Joshua, a leader who can help us defeat our enemies."

Finally there came a time when such prayers were answered, and God did send them a leader like Joshua. This time, however, the person whom God sent to help his people was not a man. It was a woman named Deborah.

Deborah was a woman prophet, or prophetess. She inspired the people and they loved and believed in her. She told them that if they would have faith in God and keep his commandments, he would help them have power over their enemies.

A general named Barak in the Israelite army was asked to lead the army against the enemy. He replied, "I won't do it unless the prophetess Deborah is at my side." He knew Deborah would cause his soldiers to feel as though they could win.

Deborah the prophetess went into battle at the side of Barak the general. Their army of ten thousand Israelites was not much of a match for the huge, well-equipped Canaanite army. But God was with the Israelites and, being inspired by Deborah, they were able to go far beyond their own

strength. Israel's inspired army was the underdog, yet it defeated its mighty enemy.

THINK ABOUT IT

1. Deborah was one of the greatest leaders of all time. Would you like to meet her sometime? Why?
2. What would you ask Deborah if you could meet her and talk to her?

A HUMBLE MAN DEFEATS THE ENEMY
Judges Chapters 6, 7

Deborah helped Israel, but after she died more trouble came. Once again the enemy armies conquered Israel. During these difficult years Israel needed more leaders like Deborah, but there weren't many others like her. God loved his people and did not want to see them so unhappy. He wanted to find leaders

with enough faith to lead his people. Finally he found such a leader—a man named Gideon. Gideon had lived a sad life because his home was located near a group of Canaanite people called the Midianites, who were a cruel, selfish people. They had often raided and stolen all the food that Gideon and his people had produced.

This good man felt sorry for his people. He had always wanted to help but had said, "What can I do about it? I'm not a strong, important leader." Because of his humble feelings he was quite surprised one day while working on his farm when an angel came to him and said, "The LORD *is* with thee, thou mighty man of valour." Gideon had never before felt that he was a mighty man.

What happened after that shows how God can help a humble man do things that others might say cannot be done. Gideon was willing to do what the Lord told him, but first he wanted to be sure the Lord was really with him; so he decided to test the Lord. The Lord went along with the test because he understood why Gideon felt as he did. Gideon said, "Behold, I will put a fleece of wool in the floor; *and* if the dew be on the fleece only, and *it* be dry upon all the earth *beside*, then shall I know that thou wilt save Israel by mine hand, as thou hast said." God did as Gideon had said "for he [Gideon] rose up early on the morrow, and . . . wringed the dew out of the fleece, a bowl full of water." Gideon still was not satisfied. One more time he asked for a sign, this time just the opposite—dry wool and a wet ground. Again God accepted the challenge. "And God did so that night: for it was dry upon the fleece only, and there was dew on all the ground." Gideon was now convinced. With God to help him, this humble farmer was willing and ready to become "a mighty man of valour."

Gideon sent word to all the people round about. He probably said, "I am willing to fight the Midianites but I need help." Thirty-two thousand men came to be in his army. When these men came, Gideon asked, "How many of you are afraid?" Some twenty-two thousand said they were. God told Gideon to send those who were afraid back home. The task that was ahead could only be done by brave men who believed. That left Gideon with an army of only ten thousand. As the soldiers marched along, they became thirsty. When they came to a stream, the Lord told Gideon to watch how the men got a drink of water. Some of them laid down on their stomachs to drink. Others knelt down and, while watching for the enemy, scooped water up with their hands. Those who had laid down were not alert, so the Lord told Gideon to send them home. Only brave, alert soldiers could do that which needed to be done. In all only three hundred soldiers were not sent home.

Gideon, with his three hundred brave, alert men, went to meet the Midianite army. By the time they arrived it was night. In the darkness Gideon crept as close as he could to an enemy camp. There he heard a Midianite say, "I had a dream that a man named Gideon would defeat us." When Gideon heard what this man said, he knew again that the Lord was with him.

Gideon returned and gathered his three hundred men around him. He told them of the ideas God had given him about how to attack. When all was ready, Gideon gave a quiet order. The little army, with God as their real captain, swept silently through the darkness toward the large Midianite army.

When Gideon and his men were very close to the enemy guards, all three hundred of them blew as hard as possible on their trumpets. Then they waved their lamps and broke their water pitchers, which made a great noise. Imagine how you would have felt if you had been a Midianite soldier and had been awakened by all those loud, strange sounds, and then through sleepy eyes had seen all those lights. It would surely have frightened anyone! And that is exactly what happened. The Midianites were soon in a panic and began killing each other, thinking their own soldiers were the enemy. The morning sun

revealed thousands of fallen Midianites, Gideon, the humble farmer, had obeyed the Lord, and with three hundred alert, brave men had won a war. He was truly "a mighty man of valour."

THINK ABOUT IT

1. What does the story of Gideon teach us about life's problems?
2. What does it mean to be a mighty person of valour?

PREVIEW OF THINGS TO COME

As we leave successful Gideon in Volume Three, we introduce in Volume Four someone who could never be considered even slightly successful. His name is Samson—big, handsome, promising Samson. We will thrill at his adventures: how he kills a lion with his bare hands, defeats an army with the jawbone of a donkey, carries off an enormous gate, gets a haircut, and finally pulls down a building. We will see him do everything except what God asked him to do.

Beautiful Ruth comes next, who is converted and moves to a new land. We learn how Boaz becomes her husband and together they start a family into which Jesus Christ will eventually be born.

Samuel is lent to the Lord by his grateful mother. God speaks to this boy and he becomes a mighty prophet. We will read of his work and how he chooses two great kings.

We will have high honor for Saul but then will be disappointed as we see him fall because of his disobedience.

Finally, a humble boy named David will defeat a giant and become one of the greatest kings to ever live.

Volume Four will indeed be a true adventure in victory and defeat, success and failure, and misery and joy. Most of all it will renew our faith in the fact that God truly is in command.